Swear Words II: More Swearier!

An Adult Coloring Book

Jennifer Conley

Swear Words II: More Swearier!

Swear Words II: More Swearier!

Copyright © 2018 Jennifer Conley

All rights reserved.

ISBN:1718861389
ISBN-13:978-1718861381

Draw your favorite swear word/phrase here and send me a pic of it!

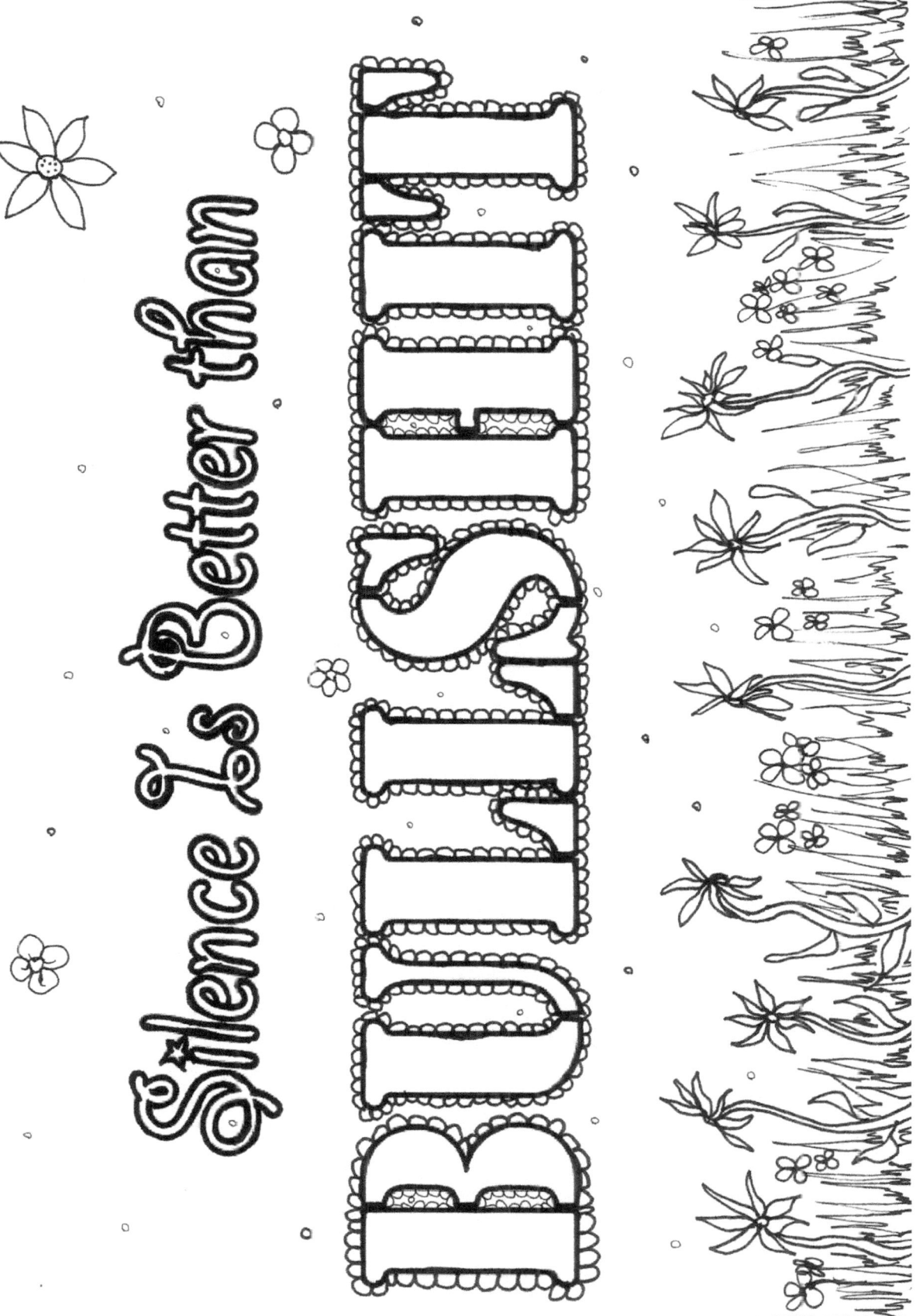

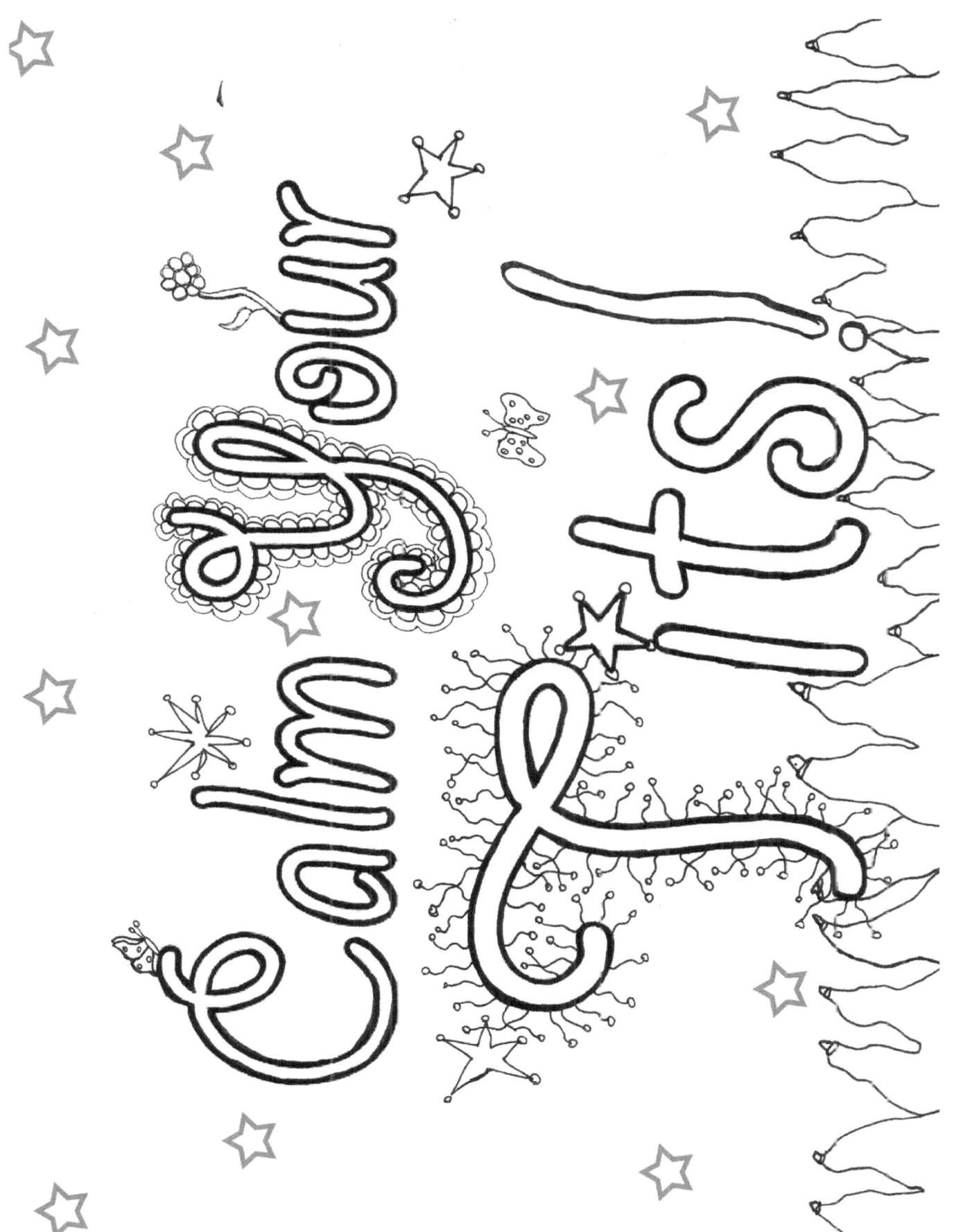

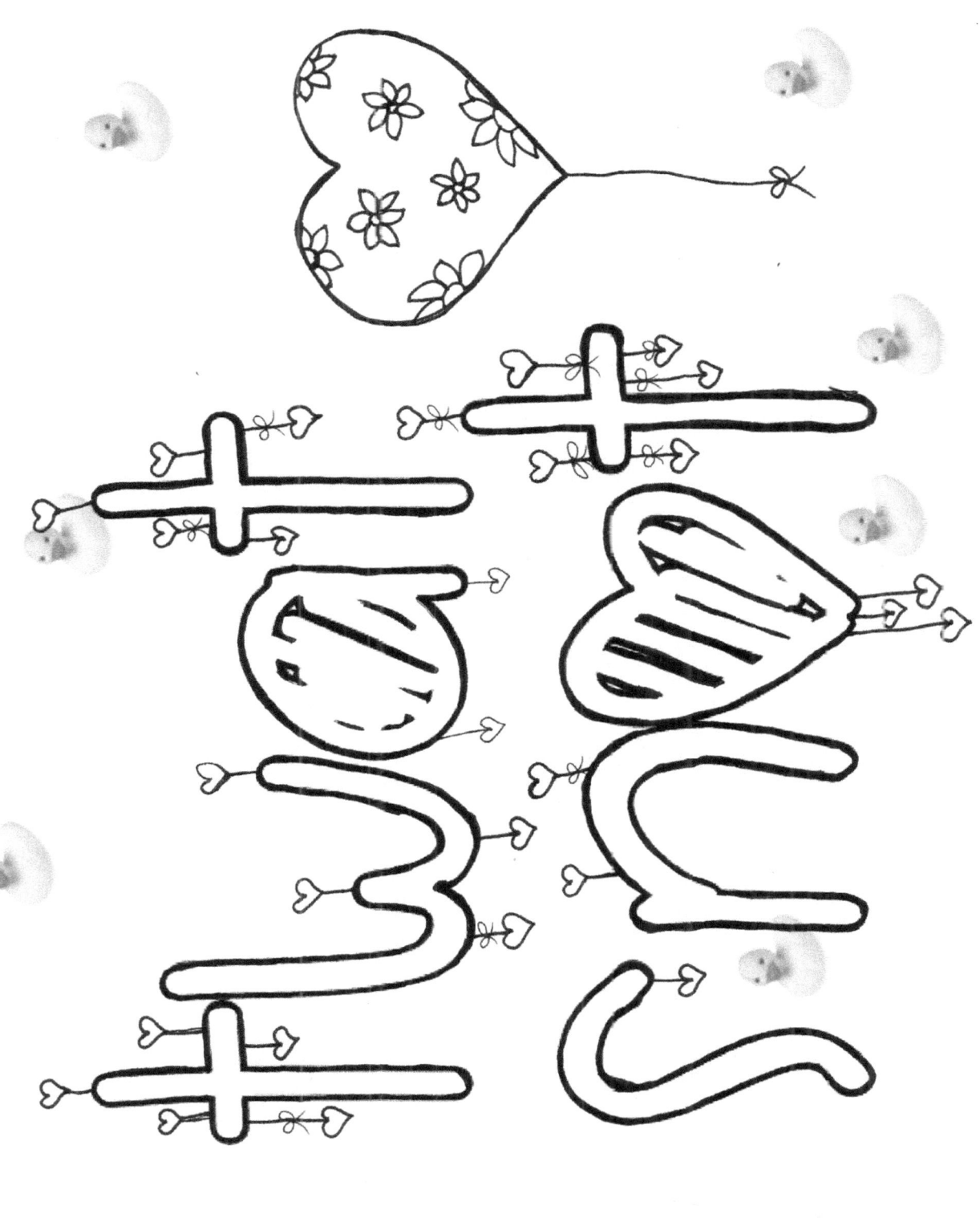

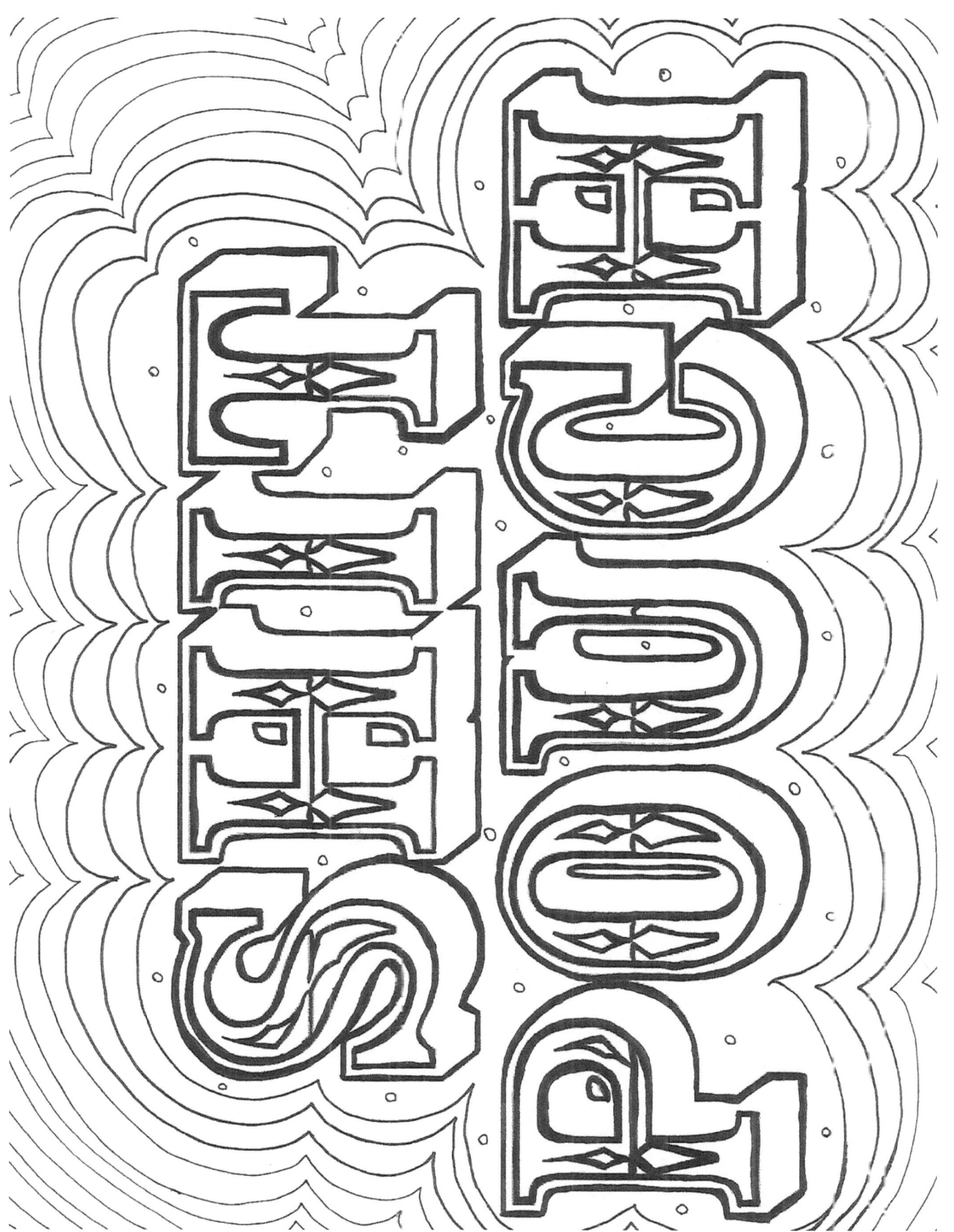

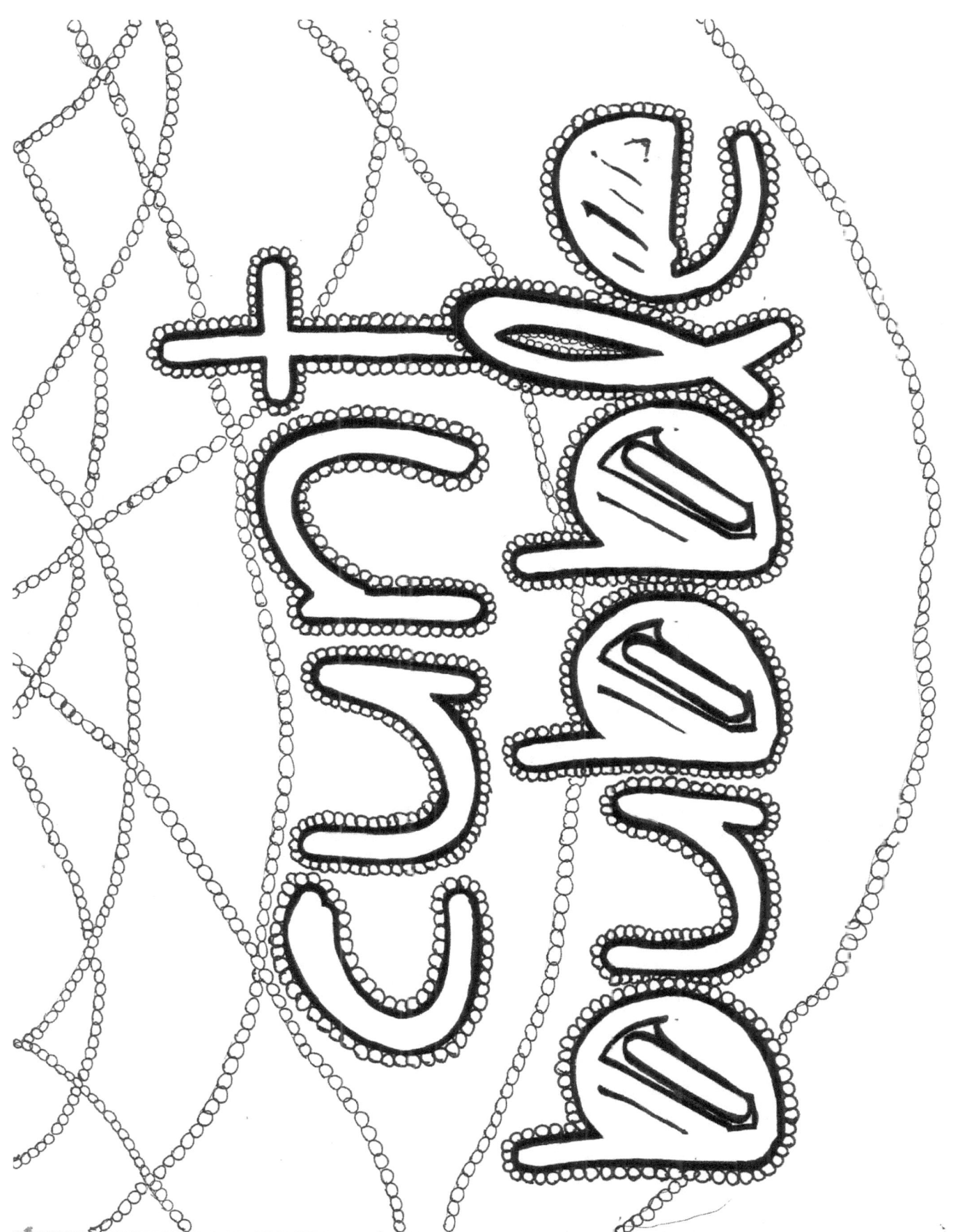

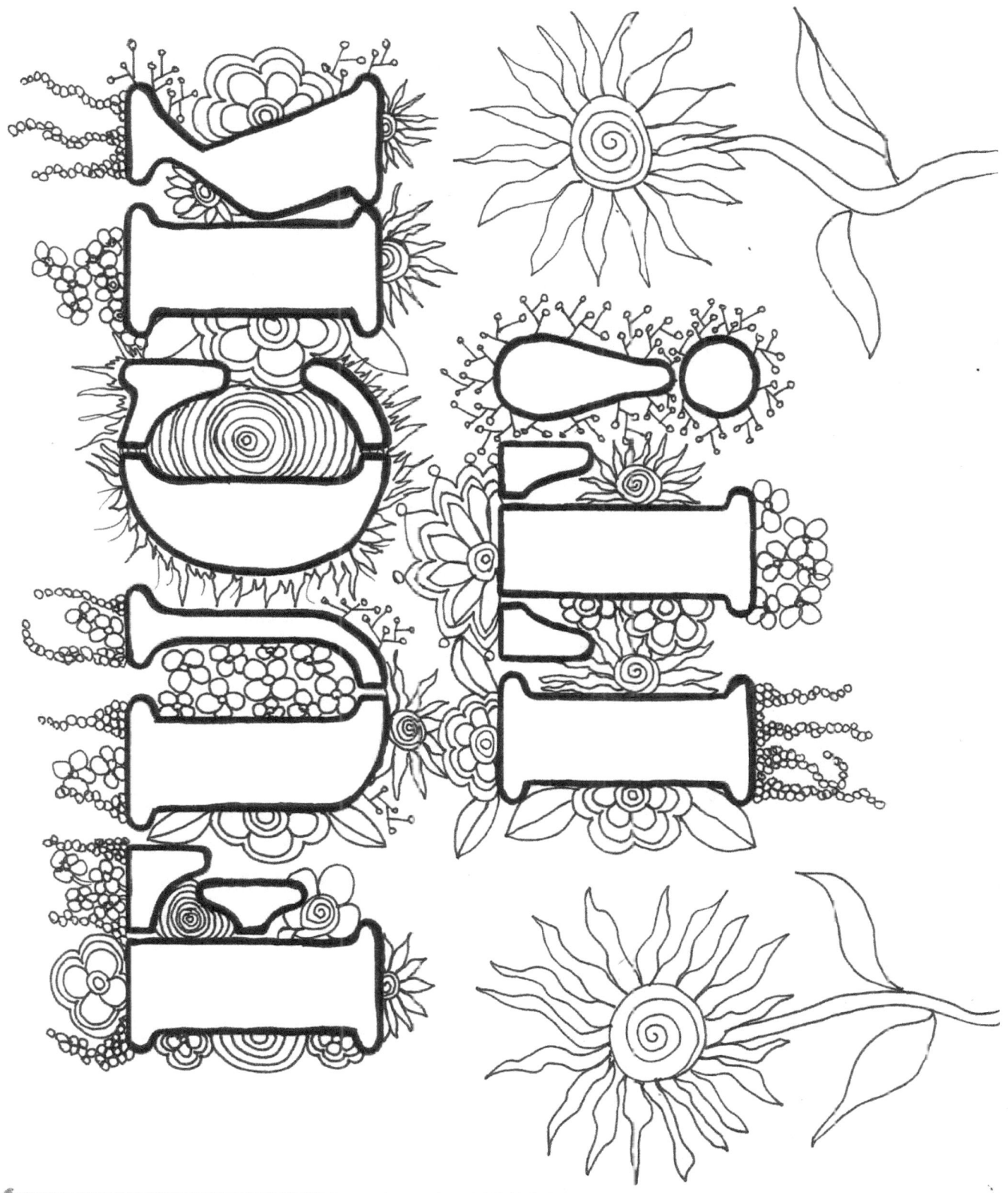

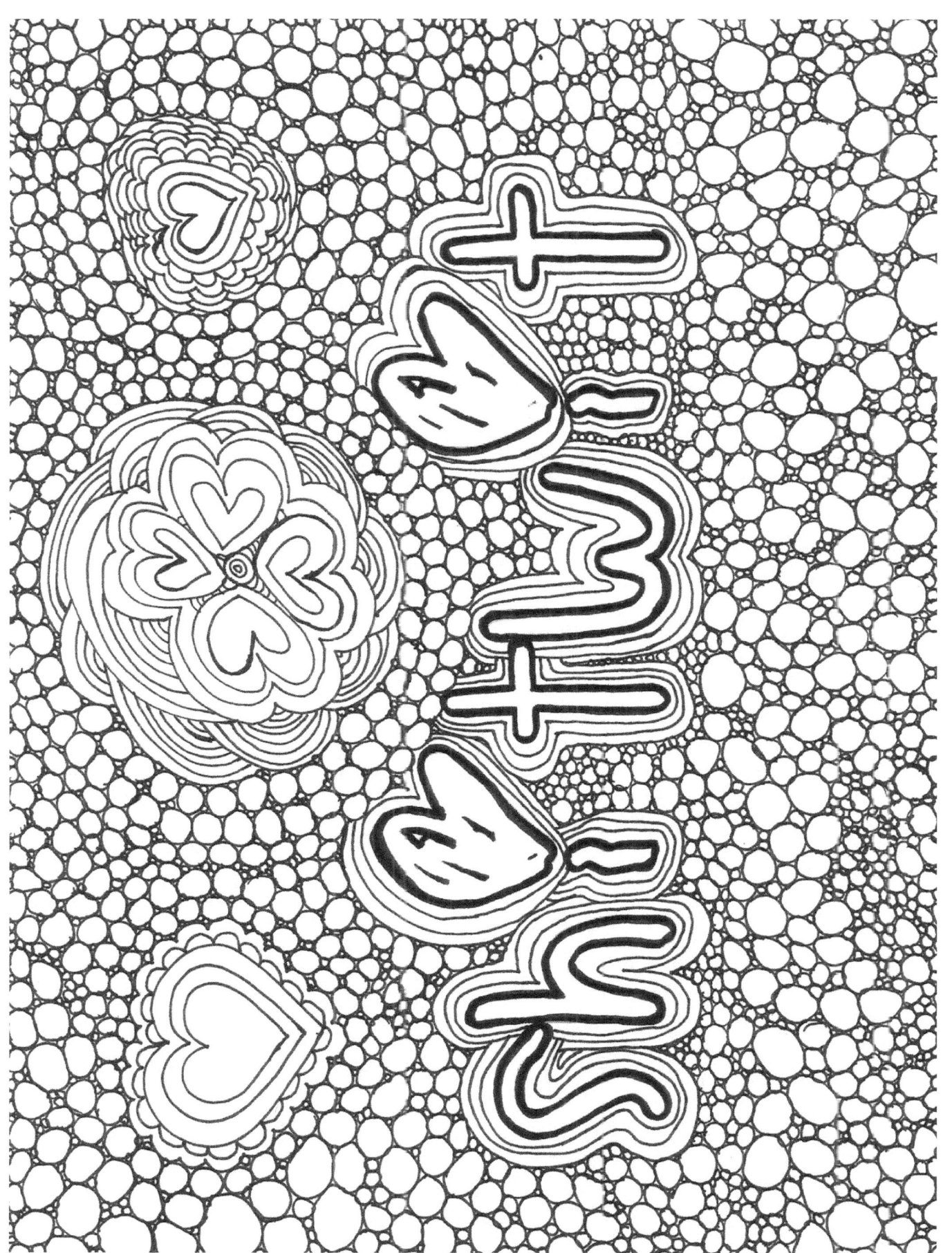

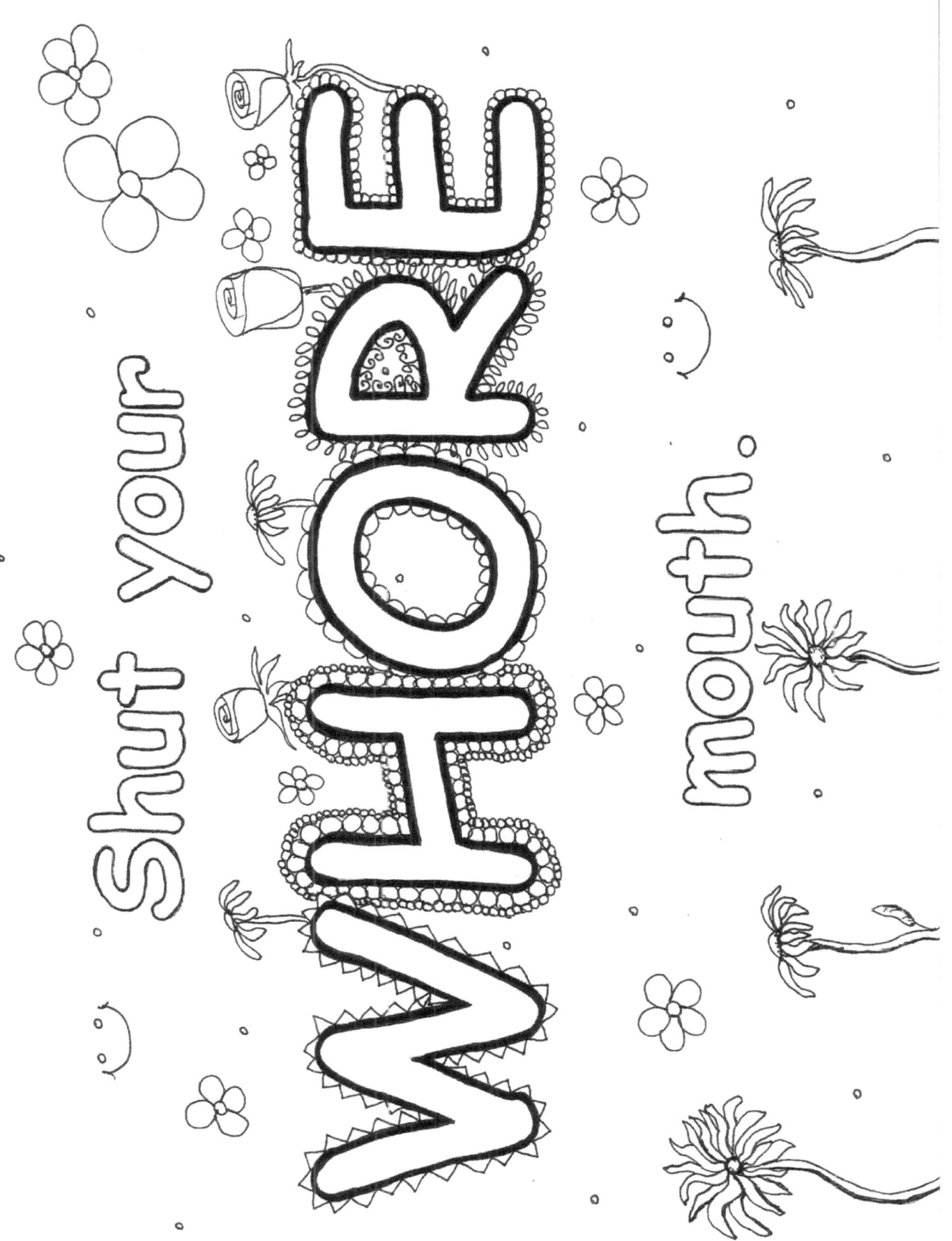

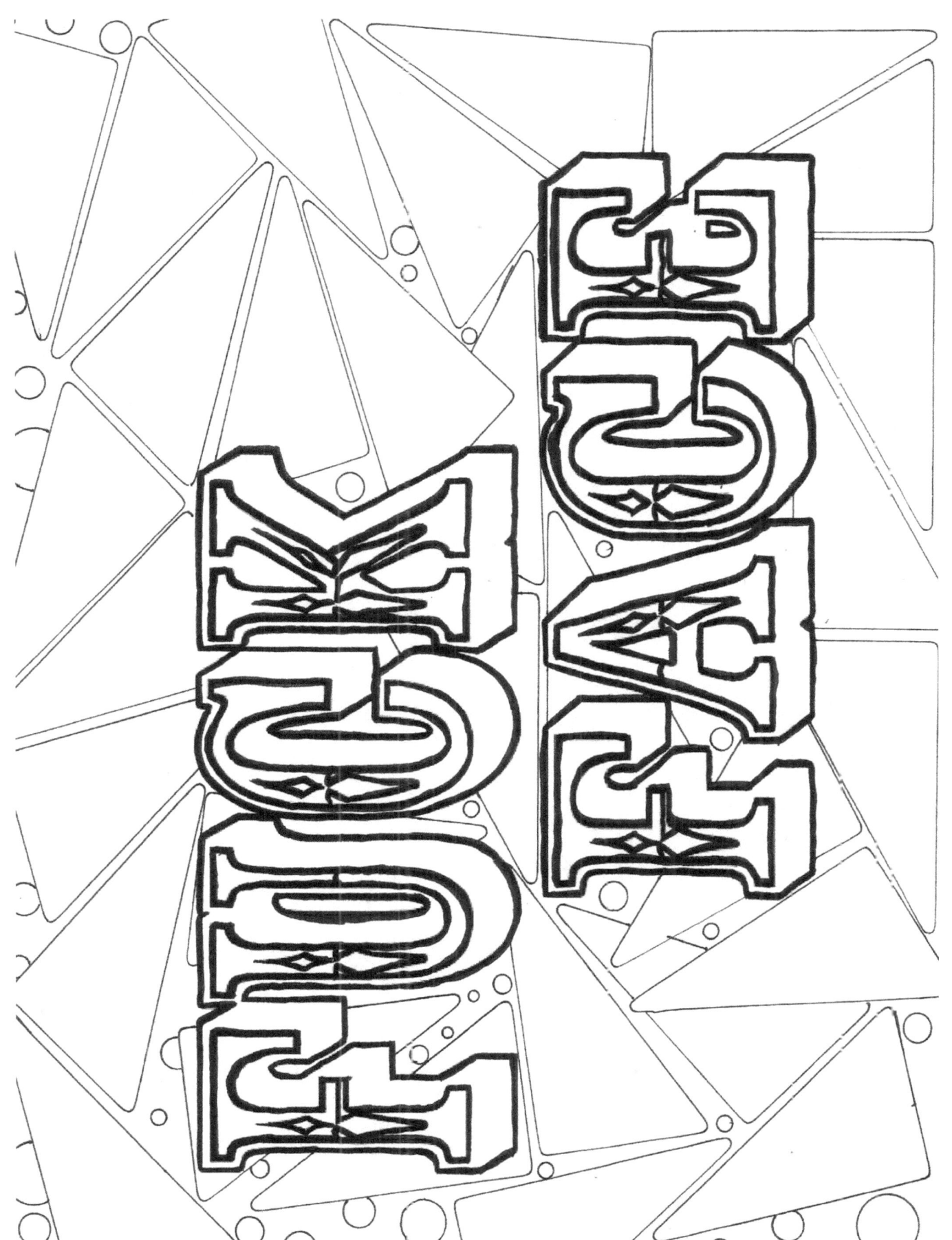

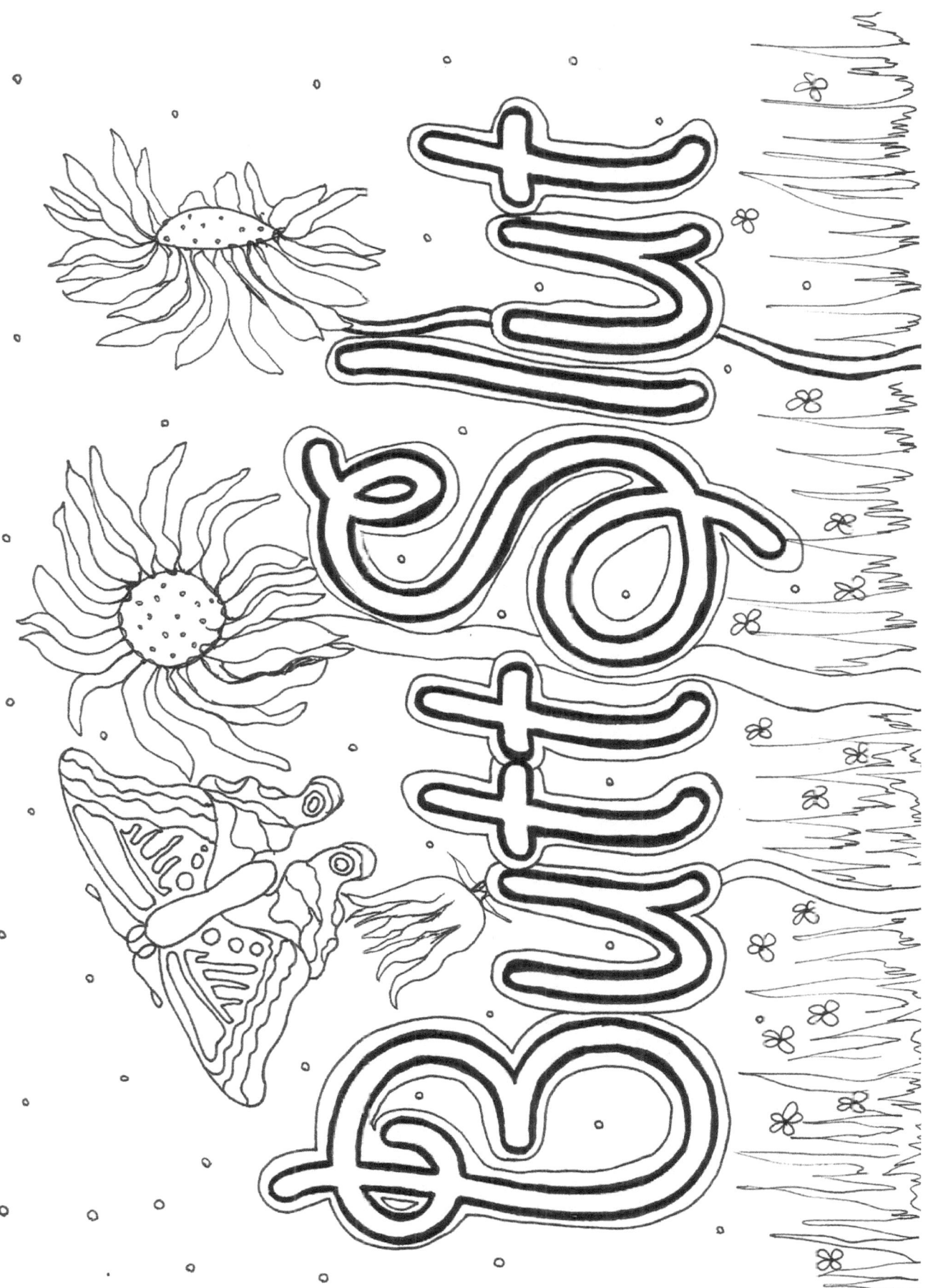

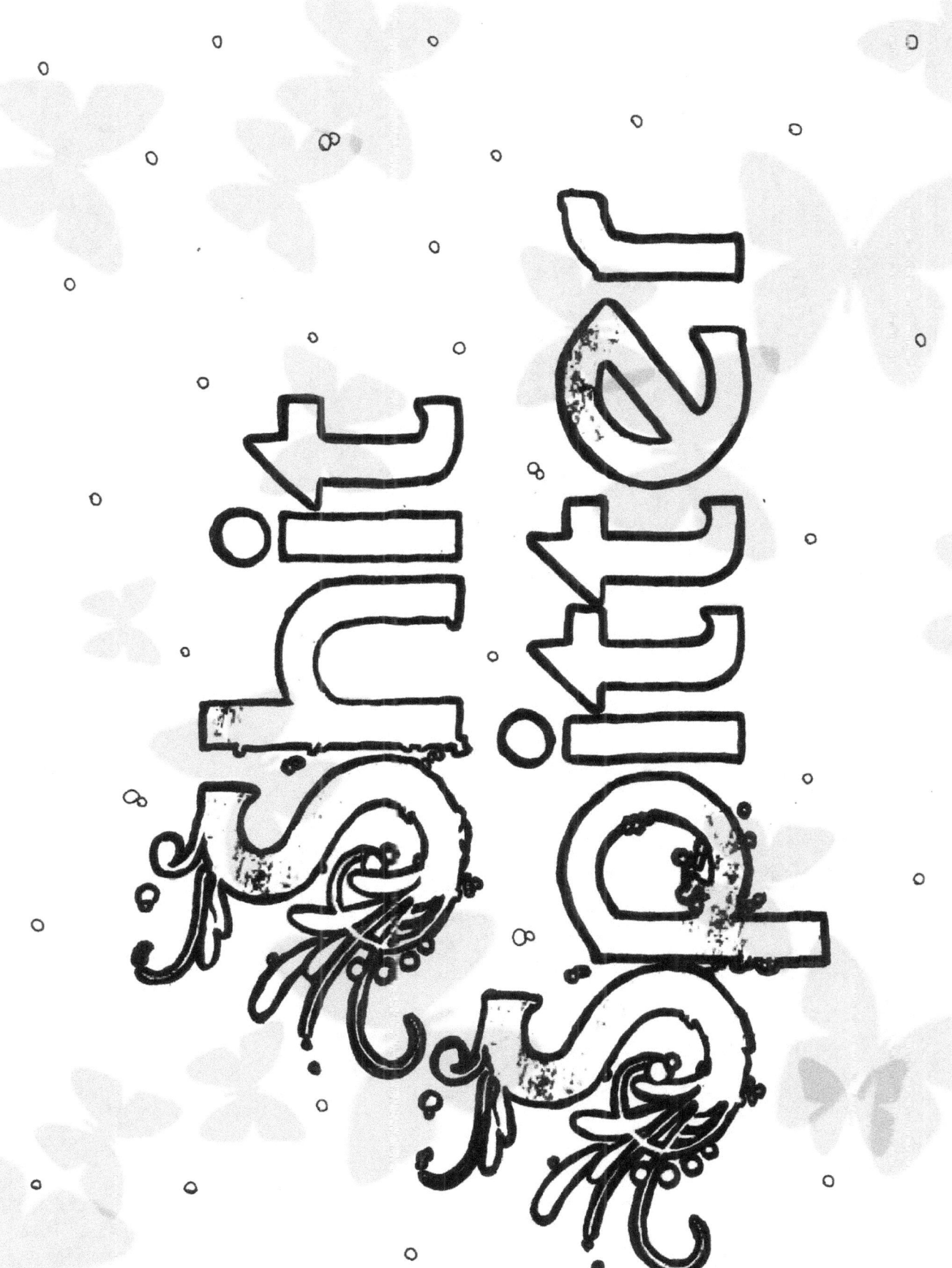

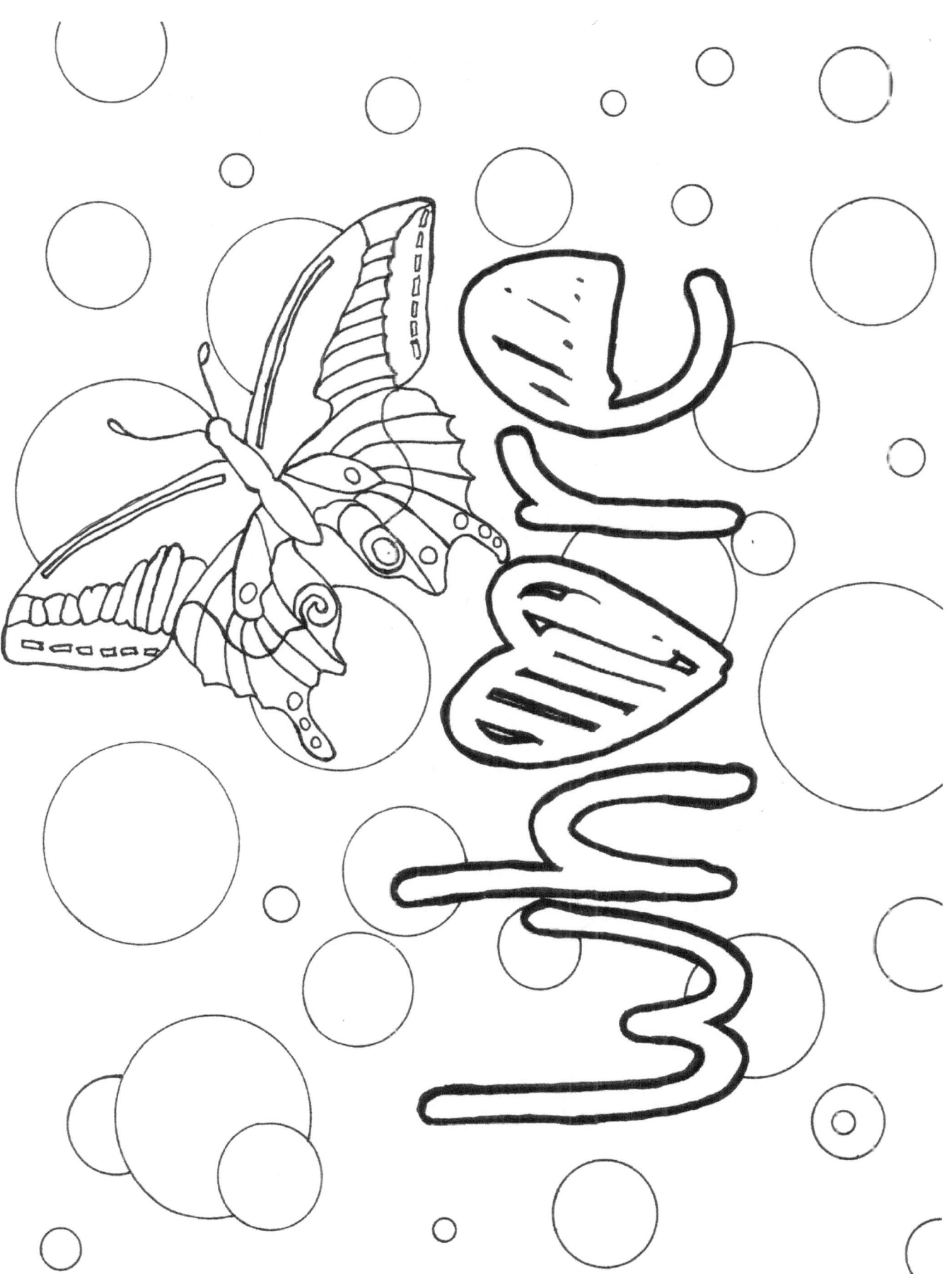

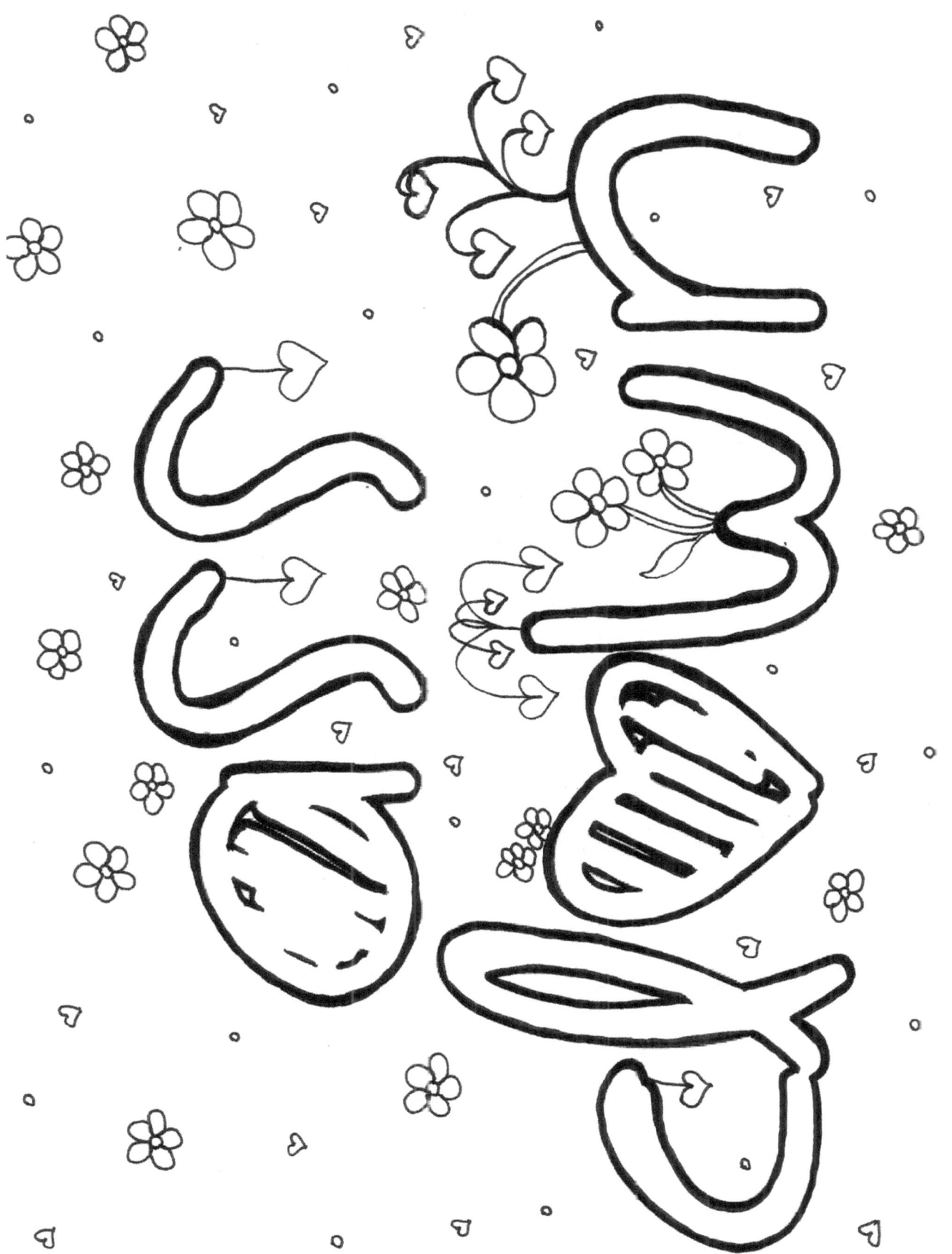

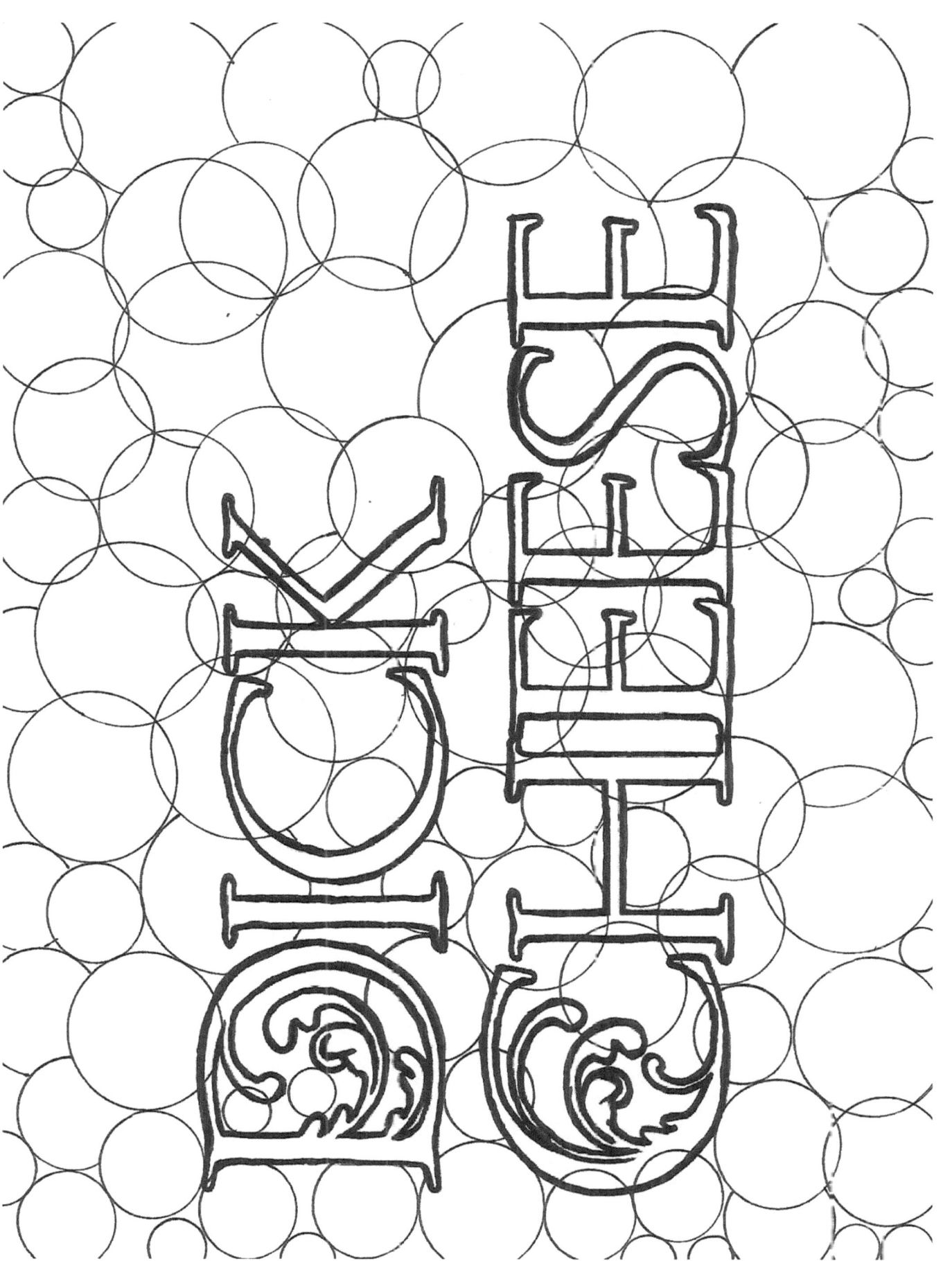

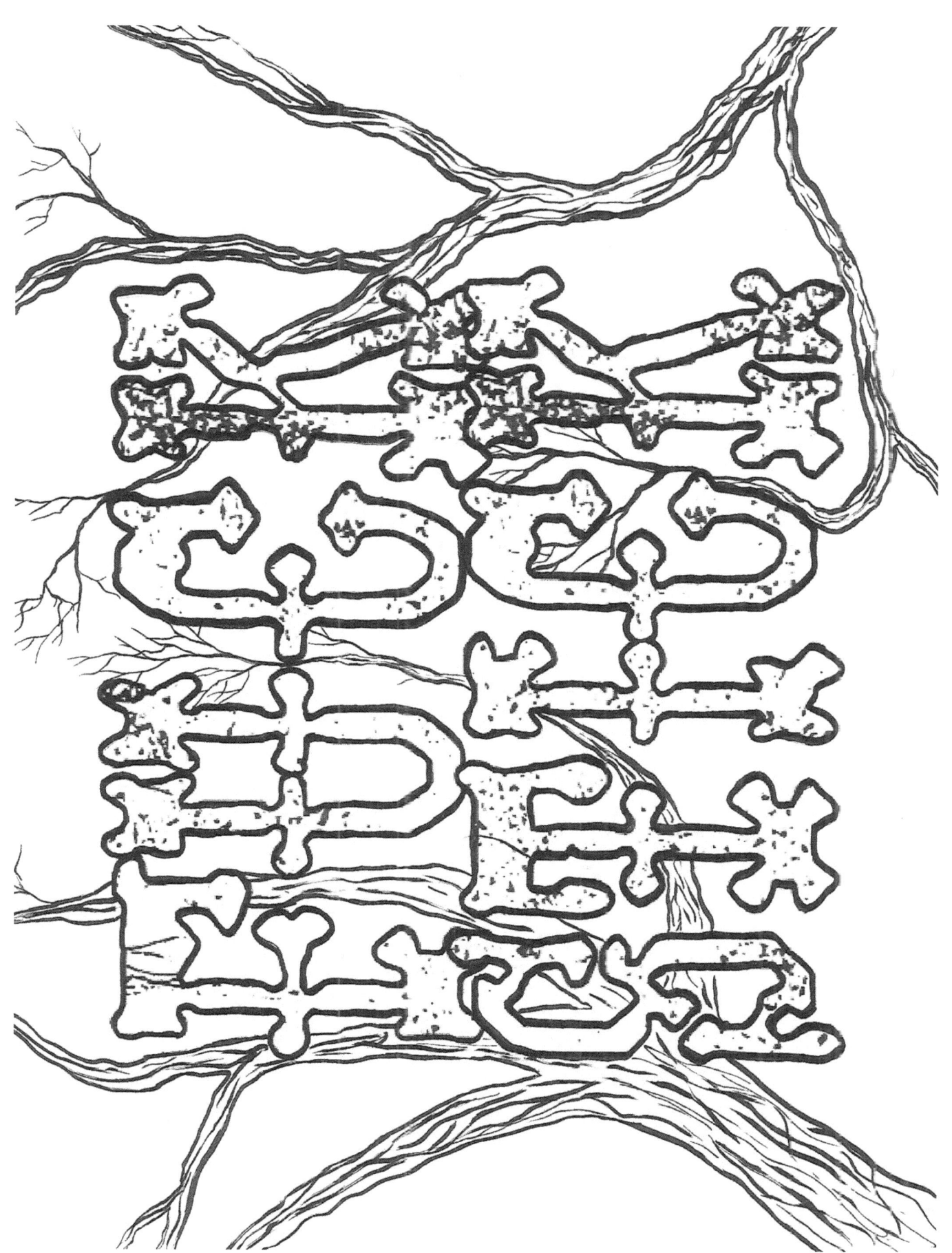

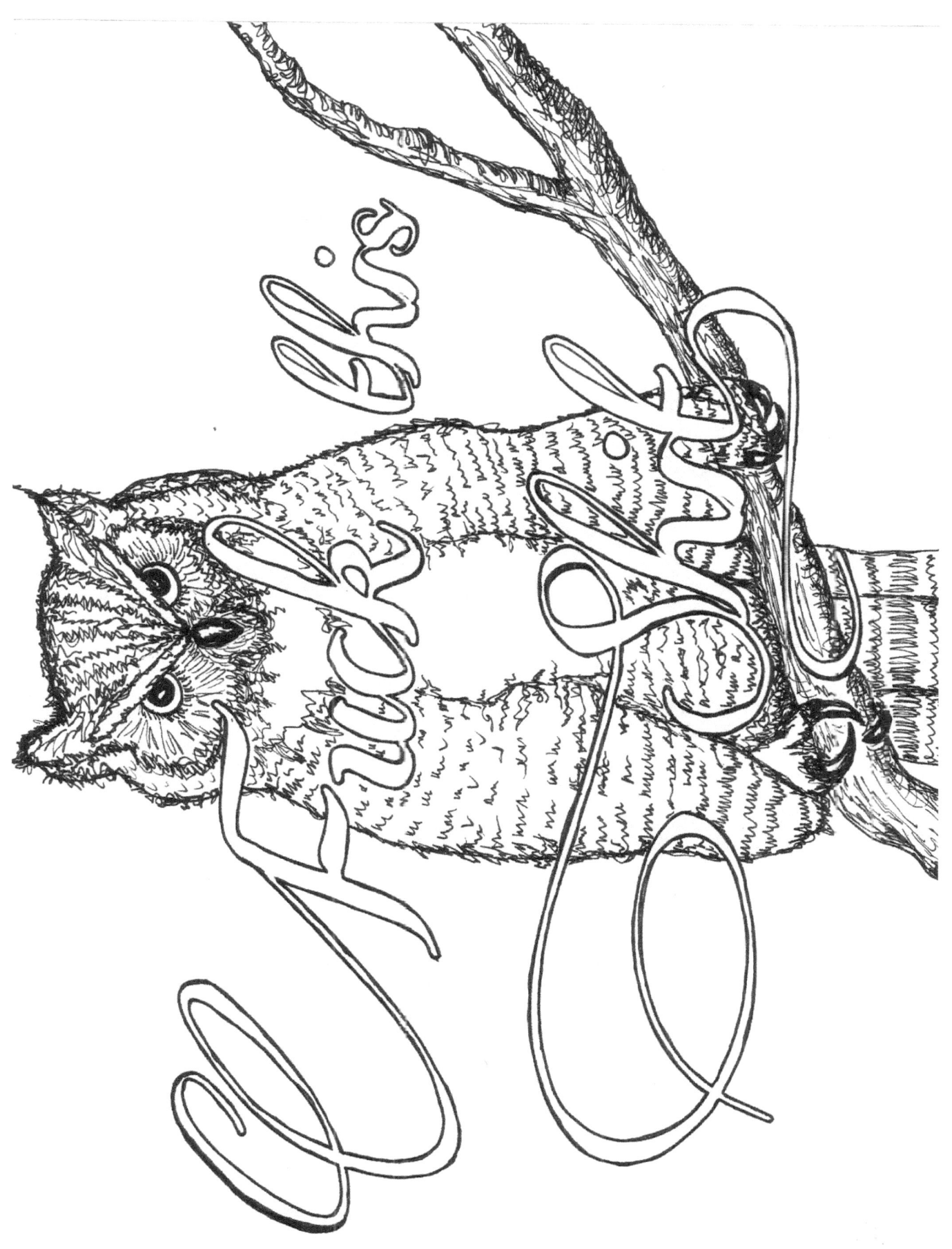

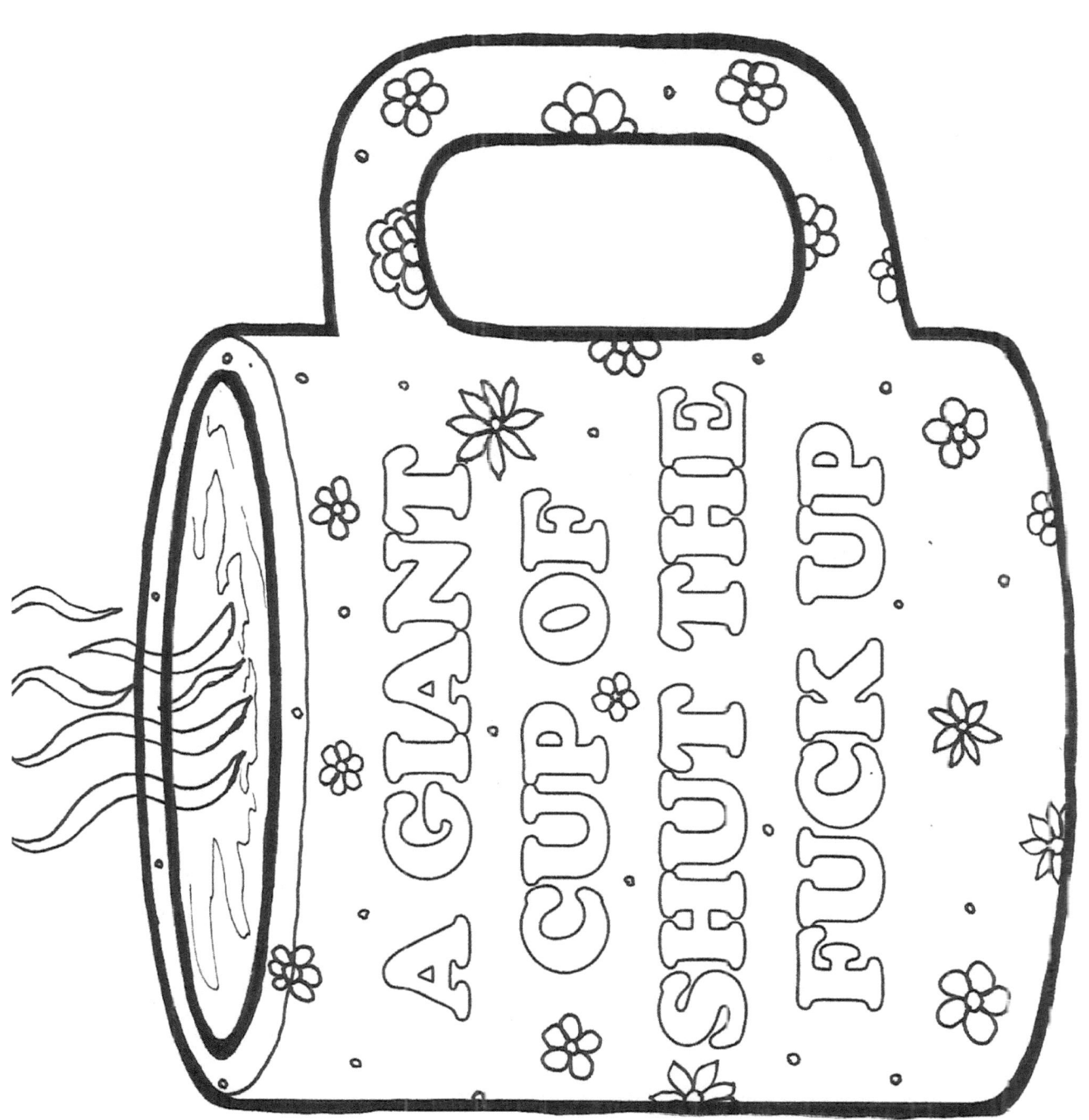

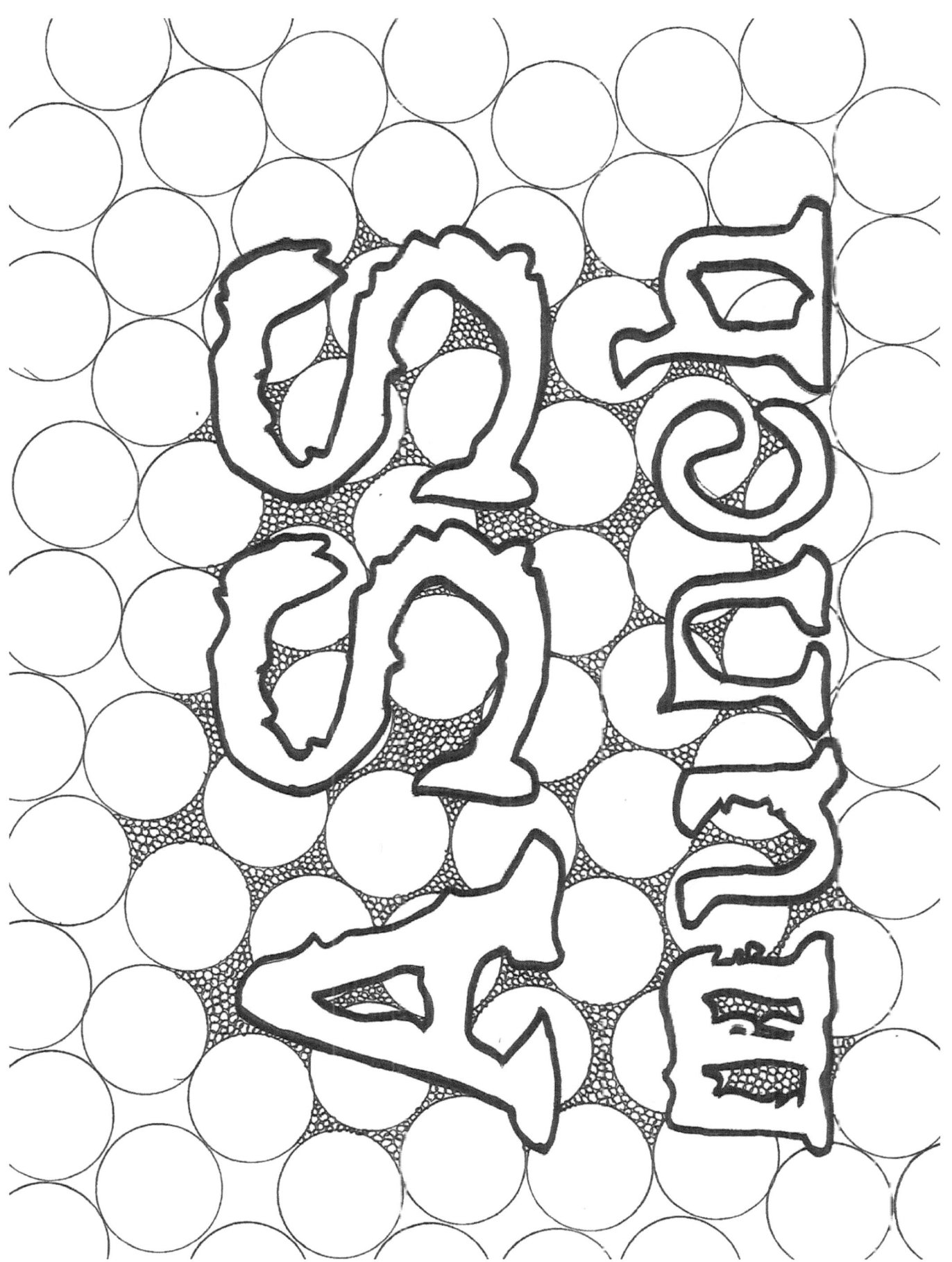

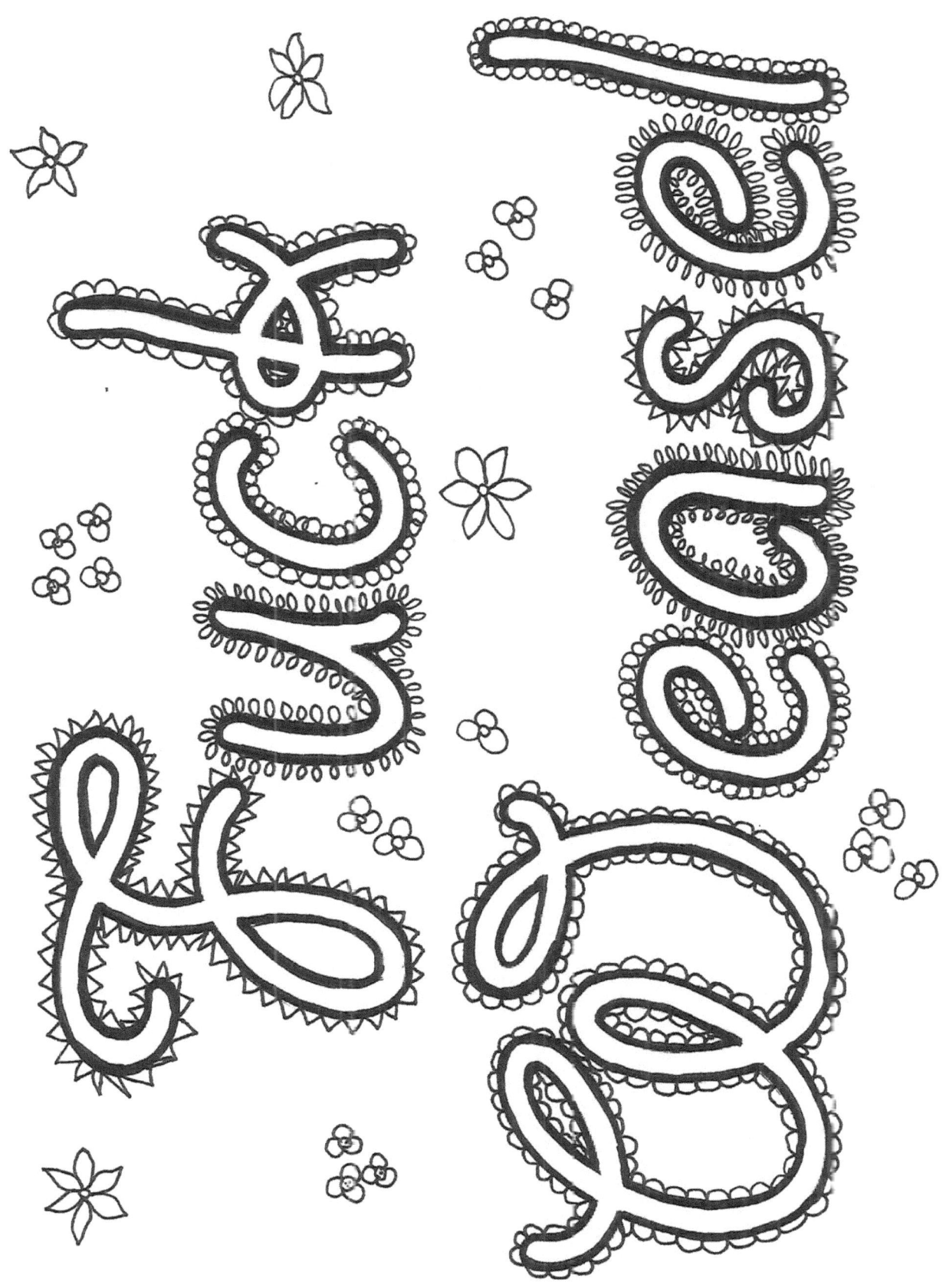

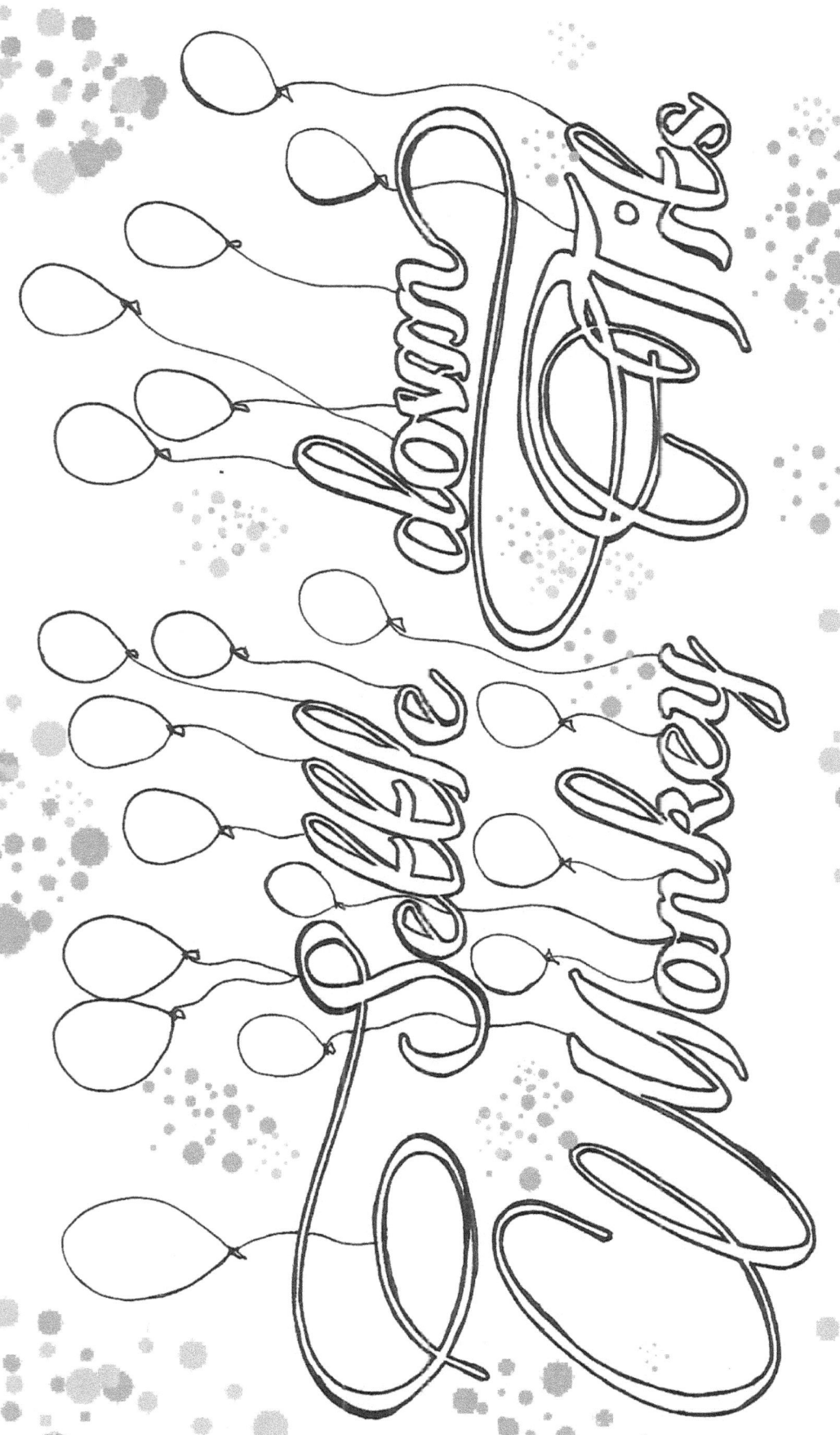

ABOUT THE AUTHOR

Jennifer Conley is an artist and author from South Jersey. In addition to Swear Words II: More Swearies!, her titles include Swear Words! An Adult Coloring Book, Mandala-Inspired Adult Coloring Book, and a children's book she wrote and illustrated called, "The Adventures of Trent & Po". You can find her original art on her Facebook page, B Inspired, (Facebook.com/JennConleyBInspired).